Cutter Class

Flowers for Australian Cake Decorating

By Gail Dorter
Photography by Stephanie Barnes

First Edition 1987
Second Edition 1988
Third Edition 1989
Fourth Edition 1990

Printed by Lamb Printers Pty. Ltd.
Perth Western Australia

Typesetting by Typestyle
Perth, Western Australia

Artwork and Design
Bruce Gordon
Perth Western Australia

Photography by Stephanie Barnes

Copyright © Gail Dorter, 1987

Author, Gail Dorter
P.O. Box 79
Hillarys, Perth, Western Australia

National Library of Australia
ISBN 0 7316 0247 1

*Bright red Gumpo Azalias crown this Christmas Bell,
along with Crowea and Holly leaves and berries. A ring of
Holly lace adds the final touch.*

About the Author

Author Gail Dorter has a background which eminently suited a lifelong ambition to decorate cakes. Her mother was a florist, and at 10 years old, Gail, along with her brother and sister had a thriving business making artificial flowers for corsages. However, it was not until 1981 that she found time to enroll in cake decorating classes, and joined the Cake Decorators Association of Western Australia.

Through a small local competition she met Sue Wells who prompted her to enter the 1981 Perth Royal Show. She did very well, and with this early encouragement has since gone on to win two Blue Ribbons, as well as five successive gold medals in the prestigious Le Salon Culinaire competitions. There have been numerous other awards along the way. In between, Gail has found time to manage her family life, conduct classes and demonstarations, as well as learning floristry. Her fresh flower bouquets are becoming as sought after as her cakes.

Gail is ably supported by her husband Peter, who is always there to cut out a board or make pillars. His encouragement, opinions, and "engineering" skills have contributed to much of her success.

Gail has always been an individualist, which shows in her work. This book is a reflection of her refreshing approach to traditional cake decorating.

Contents

It is necessary in a book of this type to name all the flowers described within. Many are indeed lifelike, while some bear only a passing resemblance to their namesakes. I hope Mother Nature will forgive me.

All the cakes flowers and ornamental pieces pictured in this book are the work of Gail Dorter.

5

Foreword

In my position of teaching cake decorating in Western Australia over many years, I have been privileged to meet and work with a great number of talented people. When I first met Gail five years ago, I knew that a gifted and dedicated lady was about to change many areas of conventional cake decorating in Australia. This book is the culmination and reflection of Gail herself - full of exciting vitality, imagination and superb artistic talent.

Over the years we have taken pleasure in hand moulding all our flowers and decorating cakes in a traditional tiered fashion. We have come to recognize and accept that new and original ideas abound in all aspects of cake decorating and that new equipment now obtainable enables the standard of our efficiency to rise to a far higher level, giving a professionalism that is essential in the continuing development of sugarcraft.

Each flower in this book is a spontaneous source of joy and pleasure to look at and to create. Once you have tried 'Gail's method' you will think about cutter flowers in an entirely new way, as part of your own creativity to make each flower with the realism nature intended.

Many will appreciate the diverse possibilities in each cake presented in this book not only the enthusiast who is exhibition minded but also the newcomer who, from ths onset has the opportunity to learn a new and easy to follow method of flower making. With practice, cutters give speed and efficiency to create perfect flowers and eliminate any failures.

The method of cutter flowers used in this book will create a tradition for many years to come.

It is my privilege to recommend this book.

Helen Bennett,
Perth,
Western Australia

Mirabilis, Daisies and Heath.

7

Introduction

In 1981 I began a course in cake decorating. Like all beginners I couldn't wait to try all the equipment I found in the various shops. Like many others, I bought cutters and went home to consult my cake decorating books for instructions. There were none. Not wanting to appear beaten before I had even started, I spent days at a time making dozens of flowers, until I discovered a use for each cutter. Then I found that other decorators were interested in my methods, and I began demonstrating my techniques.

Much controversy exists over "cutter flowers" versus "pulled" and "moulded" flowers. My answer is simple. There is room, and a place, for both.

Many potentially good cake decorators give up when they find mastering pulled flowers impossible. It is a knack that just seems to elude them. These otherwise talented people should not be lost to the cake decorating art, but encouraged to try this newer method. It is only the urge to constantly try new ideas, and create original cakes, that has bought cake decorating out of the kitchen, and into the spotlight as a definite art form. Cutter flowers combined with the older methods offer great scope for even more exciting advances in style and creativity. More importantly, it provides a niche for everyone, from the raw beginner to the accomplished professional.

So, whatever your status as a cake decorator, try making some cutter flowers. If your cutters are not identical to mine, use the techniques I offer anyway.

Your flowers may not be exactly the same as mine — they may just be better!

The basic aim of cutter flowers is to produce delicate and lifelike blooms. This can be achieved by initially rolling your paste fairly thin, then making the edges only, even thinner (by fluting or fingering). Care must always be taken not to handle the centres too much, as they need to be thick enough to shape and support the finished flower. Also, if the centres are too thin, then the green of the calyx will show through, and spoil the effect of some flowers. Again, if too thin they will split when you try to cup and shape them.

Moulding paste has been used for all the flowers illustrated (recipe page 80) as it holds its shape better than plastic icing. Always cover flowers you have cut out, as if they begin to dry, it is impossible to flute or cup them without cracking or splitting occurring.

Most small flowers use a stamen as the stem, and you may initially find it difficult making the flowers stay up. However, if you stamp out several flowers at once, by the time you have finished shaping the last one, the first should be firm enough to hold on to the stamen. Of course, climate, and the consistency of your paste also plays a part. Practice, as always, will give you a feel for when to insert the stamens. If the flowers persist in falling down the stems, simply dampen the tip of the stamen before inserting it in the flower, then hang them upside down from a piece of florists foam suspended between two objects. By the time they dry, and are finished properly with a calyx, they will be quite secure.

This cake represents a bridge between the old and the new. The throroughly modern style has a 'lavender and old lace' look about it, achieved with soft mauves and pinks on a cream background. The softly flowering sprays are made of Orchids, Eriostemon and Heath.

Tools

To successfully create flowers from cutters you will need a few basic tools.

A piece of SOFT FOAM which should be of fine consistency, and kept free of little grains of icing. BALL TOOLS of various sizes. I use such items as dressmakers pin heads, curler pins, swizzle sticks, and a melon baller — as well as commercially made ball tools. You will also need a FLUTING TOOL, such as a short length of knitting needle, or the end of a paint brush. A length of plastic piping makes an excellent ROLLING PIN. Something flat and smooth to roll the paste out on is a must. I have an acrylic board which was purchased as a "scrap" from a plastics retailer.

It is necessary to rest the flowers in or on something until they are dry. Small flowers with stamens as stems can be pushed into florists foam (OASIS). For larger flowers, you can utilise egg cartons, or cardboard fruit trays. Better still try making a HOLED BOARD.

Holed Boards

Holed boards are essential for cutter flowers, and handy for pulled ones. They allow flowers to dry while holding their shape, and are invaluable if you are transporting them any distance. They are neither difficult nor expensive to make.

Many materials can be used. As long as it is approximately 5 or 6 millimetres (¼ inch) thick, and able to be drilled, it is suitable.

Cut the board to the size you feel you need, mark where the holes are to be, and with a 6.35mm (¼ inch) bit, drill the initial holes. Use a counter sinking tool to round them out, and if necessary sandpaper any rough spots. Add legs, and it is ready for use.

My boards are acrylic, 15cm x 27cm long and 7cm high (6 in. x 11 in. and 3 in. high). For convenience I use a much smaller one for classes.

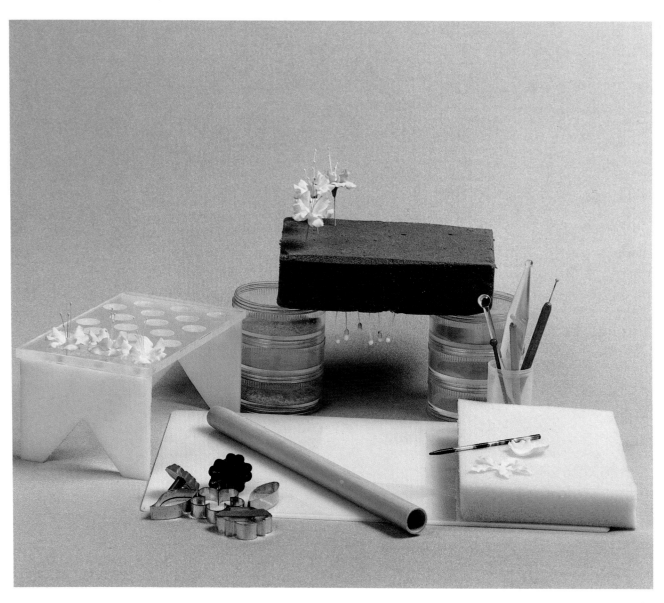

Terms used to describe techniques

FLUTE — Rest the petals on your index finger. Hold the fluting tool between the thumb and first three fingers of the other hand, and with a "roll and press" action, work around the petal. Practice will pay dividends!

FINGER EDGES — Use your thumb and fingers to gently smooth and flatten out edges, and where required, to rub chalk colouring into petals.

PAINT CALYX — Thin some royal icing with water, and colour it. Use a brush, suitably sized for the flower under construction, to paint a calyx on to the back of the flower. This not only holds the flower firmly on its stem, but when fixed into sprays, that little extra bit of green adds a natural look to arrangements. Because the flowers are neatly and realistically finished, it is not necessary to hide the backs of them, so fewer flowers are needed.

CURL EDGES — Place the flower on soft foam, and using a ball tool, gently press and pull towards the centre of the flower. Curl each petal separately, and always start at the very edge, and stop before reaching the centre of the flower.

POLLEN — Pollen adds a softening look to icing flowers, and is easily made. Simply put fresh desiccated coconut through a blender, then sift out and keep the finest particles. One teaspoon of this is sufficient for dozens of small blossoms. It can be tinted to any colour using scraped chalks. One note of warning though — if you put the coconut through the blender too long, it will be reduced to an oily consistency — totally unsuitable.

STAMENS — Both sizes of stamen are used, depending on the size of the flower. If you are just beginning on cutter flowers, use the large ones until you become adept at pulling them through without the flower sliding down the stem. I use mainly white stamens which I chalk or spray to suit my own colour schemes.

WIRE — I use very thin non rusting florist wire (26 gauge), and in most cases cover it with white or green florists tape before inserting it in the flowers.

CHALKING — Chalking, rather than painting icing flowers gives a softer more natural look. In the smaller flowers it is done last. However, in larger flowers you will achieve a better effect if it is done first, before any shaping and while the icing is soft. Dust on the powdered chalk, brush or blow off excess, and smooth it in with the thumb. Where petals are to overlap it is essential to do this before each one is put in place. Avoid using chalk "neat", always mix a little cornflour or potato flour with it to achieve an even finish. Used without cornflour it is inclined to streak.

Stamens on Stems

All flowers are easier to arrange if they are on a stem, so incorporating the centre of the flower with a stem makes sense.

Cut the stamens to the required length, and hold them in your right hand, with the stamens side by side, and the cut ends level. Rest a piece of florists tape across your left index finger, and lay the stamens over the tape, about 0.5 cm (¼ in) from the end. Use your left thumb to fold the end of the tape over the stamens, then roll them up tightly. Once secure, insert a length of 26g wire next to the stamens and continue taping down the length of the wire. Don't simply "bandage" the wire. The correct way is to twist the wire with your left hand, while gently stretching the tape with your right hand. You may find it easier if you cut the tape to half its width.

Dried cornsilk makes very realistic stamens, provided you use silk that is nice and yellow, not withered and brown, or too green. Take several strands of silk about 2.5 cms (1 in) long, and bend a piece of wire across the centre, and down into a tight hook. Tape the stem, starting right at the top so the silk is held firmly in place. Trim the stamens, and with a brush dipped in very thin royal icing tip as many ends as possible.

For a rose centre, part the stamens in the middle, and flatten them evenly round the wire stem. Pipe a dot of royal icing in the centre, sprinkle on some pollen, and shake off any excess. Dip a paintbrush in caramel or light brown liquid food colouring, and gently tip the ends of the cornsilk.

If you wish, you can dye the cornsilk, and the easiest method is to tape it on to stems ready for use, then dip the ends in food colouring, and give them time to dry. Coloured red or yellow, it is ideal for gum blossom.

If the silk becomes too dry and brittle to use, put it in a plastic bag, and spray a fine mist of warm water over it, then seal up the bag. It soon becomes pliant again, but don't leave it sealed in the plastic too long, or it reverts back to its original form.

Moulds

Many flowers need to be made in a mould to help establish their shape. It is possible to buy some commercially made forms, but it is easy and inexpensive to make your own.

Firstly, transfer the patterns from below on to a piece of stiff cardboard, or soft plastic such as the lid of an icecream or margarine container. Cut them out.

Prepare some leftover moulding paste, or childrens putty (purchased from a toy store), by pressing it into a small container, or simply make it into a block.

Gently form a hole in the centre, then use the pattern piece as a guide for the correct shape, turning it so the hole is even. The finished mould should correspond with the pattern. Round off the edges, and set aside to dry thoroughly. If you wish to preserve your mould it can be painted or sealed.

Use a ball tool to form the initial hole for Azalia or Godetia moulds, and an icing tube (nozzle) for the lilly mould. If you wish to make bigger flowers, it is a simple matter to build larger moulds.

* The idea for the use of corn silk comes from Donna Bratt of Tasmania.

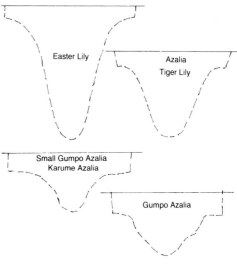

Easter Lily

Azalia
Tiger Lily

Small Gumpo Azalia
Karume Azalia

Gumpo Azalia

A large spray of Orchids on each tier is all that is needed for a very effective cake. Here they are teamed with Eriostemon and sprigs of yellow Basic Blossom to tone with the Orchids' throats

Buds

For small buds simply paint a calyx on a large stamen, using thin green royal icing. For larger buds, dip the stamen in thin royal icing, and hang upside down in a piece of oasis foam suspended between two objects. Paint on a calyx when dry. This is an ideal way to use up odd and awkward coloured stamens. Perfect holly berries can be made this way using red royal icing. If you wish they can also be dipped in edible glaze for extra shiny berries. Larger buds and berries need to be dipped twice, and allowed to dry thoroughly in between.

Basic Blossom

Roll icing thinly, cut out flowers and finger the edges. Rest the flower on your index finger and with a fluting tool roll outwards on each petal to make them finer. Remember to leave the centre area intact. Lay face down on soft foam, and using a small ball tool, press in the centre of each petal. Turn over and press in the centre to cup the flower. Wait a few minutes then push a stamen through the centre. For a better grip, slightly twist the stamen as the head goes into the icing. Stand the flower in a piece of florist's foam. When dry paint a calyx on the back, using green flood consistency royal icing. Before arranging in sprays lightly dust the centre with a deeper colour chalk. Try mixing two or three sizes together for a natural look.

If you have trouble keeping the flowers from sliding down the stems, dampen the stamen heads slightly, and hang the flowers upside down in the florists foam which has been suspended between two objects.

Boronia

Real Boronia have four petals, however, I have used both four and five petals, and no one has ever commented. Use whichever cutter you have, or whichever you find easiest.

Roll yellow paste thinly and cut out flowers. Lay the flower on your index finger and with a fluting tool roll each petal from about half its length out to the edge. Leave as much bulk in the centre as you can, but have the edges as fine as possible. Place on soft foam and curl each petal by pulling the ball tool from the petal tip, in, towards the middle. Press in the centre to cup flower. I have found a curler pin to be just the right size for this, and the flower usually curls right over almost into a ball. Insert a yellow stamen tipped with brown (either purchased as such, or tip ordinary yellow ones yourself), twisting as the head enters the icing. Paint a calyx on the back, using thin green royal icing. When completely dry use a stiff brush to chalk the outside brown. This is one of the few occasions when you can use straight chalk without diluting it with potato or cornflour.

Top Left: Green buds, taped into bunches, then taped together and airbrushed with purple colouring make the grapes for this simple but effective Father's Day Cake.

Top Right: Daisies in the guise of Dandelions lifted the otherwise 'flat' appearance of this comic cake.

14

Pink Boronia

As for brown Boronia, but use white paste, a pink stamen, and chalk the outside pink. Try these in all sorts of colours — they can be very handy when you wish to introduce a touch of very bright or deep colour.

Lily of the Valley

As for boronia, but use white paste and a green stamen. Paint small green spots on each petal if desired.

Top: Short two inch pillars help to create the cascade effect on this cake. The top tier is set to the back and one side, so the Double Blossom, Eriostemon and Heath tumbling from the tulle bell can spill onto the front of the base cake. Two gold rings nestled amongst the flowers of the top tiers.

Bottom: Two crossed wine glasses formed an unusual but appropriate feature on this rectangular cake. Pink Gumpo, Azalias, Double Eristemon and blue Coral Flowers form the sprays. Long lace pieces lend elegance to the sides.

Thryptomene

Roll paste thinly, and cut out flowers. Hold the flower on your index finger, and with a fluting tool, roll outwards on each petal to make the edges finer. Place face up on soft foam, and use a very small ball tool to slightly cup the edge of each petal. Wait a few minutes for the icing to firm up a little, before pushing a small stamen through the centre, twisting it slightly as the head goes into the icing. Set in florists foam to dry, then paint a calyx on the back using thin green royal icing. Once dry, paint a tiny spot of thin royal icing in the centre, sprinkle on some pollen and shake off any excess.

When making Thryptomene, cup some of the flowers in the centre as well, so they look to be in different stages of development and more realistic when taped into a spray.

Gypsophila

Roll white paste thinly and cut out flowers. Lay the flower on your index finger and use a fluting tool to roll from side to side on each petal, thinning and broadening the petals. Take care not to work the centre of the flower. Lay face down on soft foam, and using a small ball tool, press either side of each petal, turn over and press in the centre to cup the flower. Wait a few minutes then push a green stamen through the centre. For a better grip, slightly twist the stamen as the head goes into the icing. Stand in florists foam to dry. When dry paint a green calyx on the back using thin green royal icing. To finish, dust a little extra green chalk in the centre. These flowers look good with dark red or burgundy roses. Of course you can use colours other than green and white to make a pretty flower.

Soft pink Double Blossom cascading from a tull bell and across the front of the lower tiers set the mood for this cake. They are mixed with Eriostemon, pale pink Boronia and a few pale blue Gypsophila.

18

Basic Jasmin

Roll paste out thinly and cut out flower. Finger and neaten the edges. Place face down on soft foam and curl each petal by pulling a ball tool from the petal tips, in, towards the centre. Turn over and press in the middle. Insert a large stamen in the centre, twisting it slightly as the head goes into the icing. To finish, paint a calyx on the back using thin green royal icing. Traditionally these are white, with a white stamen, and pink on the back, but I use many colours and they are always attractive.

Realistic Jasmin

Roll white past thinly and cut out flower. Finger and neaten the edges. Place face down on soft foam and curl each petal by pulling a ball tool from the petal tips, in, towards the centre. Turn over and press in the middle to cup the flower. Insert a large white stamen in the centre, twisting it slightly as the head goes into the icing. Set in florists foam to dry. Thin some white royal icing with water, and paint it on the back of the flower and a little way down the stem to create a tubular look. Once dry chalk the backs with pink. Lastly paint on a green calyx using thin green royal icing.

To avoid air bubbles appearing in the royal icing, dry the flowers as quickly as possible. My trick is to put them in the oven with only the light on. You might also try blowing a hair dryer on them.

Buds are made by dipping further into icing than usual to give an elongated look, and chalked with pink before painting on a calyx in the usual way. These flowers can be made into separate sprays, using as many buds as flowers, then the sprays bunched together as the feature on a very feminine cake.

Top: A very simple single tier wedding cake relying on a spray of Frilled Cactus Flowers, Eriostemon, pale pink Boronia and blue Gypsophila for its impact.

Bottom: A ring of flooded 'key and ribbon' lace pieces resting against the sides create an unusual feature on this Birthday Cake. The spray which curves around the cake and cascades down the side consists of Double Blossom, Eriostemon, Heath and Forget-Me-Nots. Just a touch of apricot was sprayed round the base of the cake before decorating.

Eriostemon

Roll paste thinly and cut out flower. Lay the flower on your index finger and use a fluting tool to roll from side to side on each petal — avoid the centre of course. Place face up on soft foam and press in the middle with a ball tool. Push a large stamen through the centre, twisting as the head goes into the paste. Stand in florists foam to dry. Finish by painting on a calyx using thin green royal icing, and chalking some colour in the centre. For a delightfully different effect, try just a touch of a complimentary colour on some of the petals (not all) in each flower. When bunched together in sprays they can add that extra "something" a cake often needs.

Double Eriostemon

Roll paste very thin and cut out two pieces for each flower. Finger and neaten the edges. Lay the petals on your index finger and use a fluting tool to roll from side to side on each petal, then place on soft foam and add a touch of egg white to the centre. Roll the second set with the fluting tool and place on top of the first, alternating the petals. Press in the middle with a small ball tool, and insert a large stamen in the centre, twisting as the head enters the paste. (use up your old and odd colours as they won't show on the finished flower). When dry, paint a calyx on the back using thin green royal icing. To finish, put a small drop of thin royal icing in the centre, sprinkle on pollen and shake off any excess.

These flowers look lovely in white with virtually any colour in the centre. They are especially suitable for mauve cakes, as mauve pollen holds its colour well. Try teaming them with fruit blossom or double blossom for a delicate look.

Tubular Eriostemon

Make as for basic eriostemon, but paint and chalk the back in the same fashion as for heath or jasmin. ▶

Top: Red Gumpo Azalia, Gypsophila and cream Heath, all spilling from a tulle bell and across the front of the base cake create a simple yet dramatic effect. The two rows of ribbon and lace serve to soften the look just a little.

Bottom: Fushias, white Heath and just a few Basic Blossom in pink formed the eyecatching arrangement on this Formal Occasion Cake.

Hyacinth

Hyacinth are fleshy looking, so don't roll your paste too thin. Cut out flower, finger lightly, then press a pin down the middle of each petal to create a vein. Try not to mark the centre. Turn the flower face down on soft foam and using a ball tool, gently stroke each petal from the tip, in, towards the centre to curl the petals. Turn over, and press the ball tool in the middle to cup flower. Insert a large stamen in the centre, and pull through, twisting slightly as the head goes into the paste. Sit in florists foam until it is dry enough to paint a calyx on the back with thin green royal icing. Once dry, dust a deeper colour chalk in the centre, and along the petals to highlight the veins.

If you wish to have a more tubular looking flower, before painting on the calyx, colour some royal icing to match the flower. Thin it slightly with water, and brush it on to the back of the hyacinth and a little way down the stem.

Allow to dry, and finish with a green calyx of thin royal icing.

Opposite Page: Cascading Orchids, softened with fairly long ribbon loops, Eriostemon, and sprays of pink Basic Blossom help to create this lovely cake. The Bride and Groom plaque adds tradition to a very modern style.

Daisy

(METHOD A)

Use any daisy cutter available. If you don't have a daisy cutter, use a primula cutter, and slit each petal down the centre.

Roll paste thinly and cut out flowers. Rest the flower on your index finger, and use a fluting tool to roll from side to side on each petal, thinning the edges nicely. Place face up on soft foam, and press in the centre with a ball tool. Some petals will lift, giving a less regimented look and the centre will cup slightly. Wait a few minutes, and if it is a small daisy, insert a large stamen in the centre, twisting it slightly as the head goes into the paste. Sit in florists foam to dry before painting a calyx on the back using thin green royal icing. Finish by chalking a touch of colour in the centre, and a complimentary shade on some of the petals.

For a larger daisy, use a piece of sprayed or taped wire as a stem. Bend the tip at right angles and insert in the centre of the flower. Secure with a touch of thin royal icing. Once dry, chalk on any colour you require. Finish by dropping a spot of thin royal icing in the centre and sprinkling on some pollen. Shake off excess and set to dry in florist foam. Neaten the back with a calyx of thin green royal icing.

B

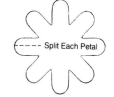

Double Daisy

Roll paste thinly and cut out two sets of petals (or three if you prefer) for each flower. Make up using either method A or B. Paint a spot of egg white in the centre of the base petals, and lay the second set on top, taking care to alternate the petals. Press firmly in the centre with a ball tool. Finish either with a pollen centre or a large stamen if the flower is only small.

When the Bride couldn't choose between a tulle bell or a Bride and Groom for her cake, I suggested having both. As the picture shows, it was a satisfactory solution. The sprays of flowers consist of mauve Double Blossom, Eriostemon, and sprigs of pale Boronia.

A
METHOD B

Roll paste very thinly. Cut out flowers and finger any rough edges. Place face down on soft foam, and use a ball tool to gently press from the tip of each petal, in, towards the centre. Turn over and press in the centre to slightly cup the flower. Finish as for method A.

NB . . . Daisy petals break off easily as you are arranging them, especially larger ones. To counter this, cut a calyx out of thinly rolled green paste (a blossom cutter is ideal). Use a little egg white to attach to the back of the daisy. To be effective the calyx must extend a little way down the petals to support them. You can attach it at any stage of making.

Coral Flower ✿

These flowers are naturally bright red, and very handy for Christmas cakes. However, they look beautiful in any colour, so you can let your imagination go!

Colour the paste, roll out thinly and cut out flowers. Cover those you are not working on. Lay the flower on your index finger, and use a fine fluting tool to roll the petals from the centre, out to the tips. Take care to avoid the middle of the flower. Lay on soft foam and use the smallest of ball tools to press in the centre, then gently roll it around to cup the flower. Insert a small stamen in the centre, and allow to dry in florist foam. When set, colour royal icing to match the flower, thin slightly with water, and use a brush to paint the icing on the back of the flower and a little way down the stem. Once dry, paint on a green calyx with thin royal icing.

Forget-Me-Not

This tiny little flower can be used to enhance any colour scheme, or if necessary, alter it.

Where a finished arrangement doesn't quite have the overall colour you require, try adding forget-me-nots. Even large numbers of them can be dotted through an arrangement without changing, or spoiling the line. I usually make them in deep colours, as they tend to disappear if they are paler than the rest of the flowers. Blue forget-me-nots, sprinkled through pink flowers on a bridal cake add a touch of tradition.

Roll paste very thin, and cut out flowers. They dry quickly, so cover the ones you are not working on. Lay the flower on your index finger, and use a fine fluting tool to roll the petals from the centre, out to the tips. Leave as much bulk in the middle of the flower as possible. Lay on soft foam, and use the smallest of ball tools (a dressmakers coloured pinhead is ideal), to press in the centre, then gently roll it around to really cup the flower. Insert a small stamen, and sit to dry in florist foam. Finish by painting a calyx on the back using thin green royal icing.

Top: White Fast Open Roses with cornsilk centres, Eriostemon and sprigs of blue Basic Blosom trail down the side of the fan on this Silver Anniversary Cake, which echoed the style of the clients original wedding cake.

Bottom: Frangipanis, Eriostemon, sprigs of Basic Blossom and a few Forget-Me-Nots adorn this cake for Helen. Templates were pinned to the sides before spraying lightly with pink for an interesting effect on the side.

Primula

Roll paste thinly, and cut out flowers. Lay the flower on your index finger, and use a fluting tool to roll from side to side on each petal, broadening and thinning at once. Avoid working the very centre of the flower. Place face up on foam and use a ball tool to press firmly in the centre to cup the flower and lift the petals. Insert a stamen in the centre — for a better grip, slightly twist the stamen as the head goes into the paste. Stand in oasis foam to dry before painting on a calyx using thin green royal icing. Once the calyx has dried, use chalk to highlight the centre with a deeper colour. If you are making large primula dry them on a holed board or you will find that the stems will bend with the weight of the flowers.

Crowea

The centre of this flower is made by using waste pieces of stamens.

Tape six pieces on to a stem before rolling icing and cutting out flowers. Finger lightly, then press a pin down the middle of each petal to create a vein. Try not to mark the centre. Turn the flower face down on soft foam and using a ball tool, gently stroke each petal, from the tip, in, towards the centre to curl the petals. Turn over and press the ball tool in the middle to cup the flower. Colour some royal icing to match the centre of the flower, thin with water, and paint it sparingly from just above to just below the tape holding the stamens. Push the stem into the centre of the flower and pull through to the stamens, so no tape shows. Set in a holed board to dry before painting a calyx on the back, using thin green royal icing.

Trim the stamens if necessary, and use very thin royal icing in a deep colour to paint the tip of each stamen. A centre chalked in green, and red tipped stamens looks great with holly leaves and berries on a Christmas cake.

Double Blossom with Holly leaves and berries around an unrolled parchment make a simple Christmas Cake. The flooded bells with holly lace that surround the cake are very easy to manage if you handle the pieces by the flooded portion.

30

Heath 🌼

Roll paste thinly, cut out flowers and finger the edges. Hold the flower on your index finger and with a fluting tool roll outwards on each petal to make them finer. Remember to leave the centre area intact. Lay face down on soft foam, and using a small ball tool, press in the centre of each petal. Turn over and press in the centre to cup the flower. Wait a few minutes then push a stamen through the centre. For a better grip, slightly twist the stamen as the head goes into the paste. Stand in florists foam to dry. Colour royal icing to match the flower and thin slightly with water. Use a brush to paint the royal icing on to the back of the heath and a little way down the stem. When this is dry chalk on any colour desired and paint on a calyx using thin green royal icing. These flowers are very handy "fill-ins". Buds are made by dipping stamens further into the royal icing than normal. Cream coloured heath used with red main flowers on a cake will reduce the stark look.

NB . . . . To avoid air bubbles appearing in the royal icing after it is painted on, it is necessary to dry the flowers quickly. I paint the backs on only a dozen at a time before placing them in a warm place to dry.

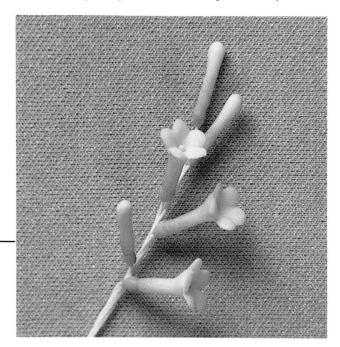

Lantana 🌼

Lantana come in some lovely bright colour combinations as well as white. If you have access to real lantana study the various shades before you begin colouring your paste. You can also invent your own "hybrids".

For Lantana make Heath (above) in two colours, such as orange and red, gold and orange, or cream and pink. Make the tubular extension on the back very fine and not too long. Finish with the green calyx in the usual way.

Make some very small buds by painting a calyx on stamens. If possible use stamens with very fine stems for both the buds and flowers.

Start by taping a bunch of five or six buds on to a wire stem about 1 cm down from the tips. Cut off the excess stamen stems before adding a circle of flowers around, and slightly higher than the buds. Again, cut off the excess stems, before adding another row of flowers. Cut off the excess stems of the last row, then continue taping down the wire. Finally, use tweezers to push and coax the flowers into place. You will need between ten and fourteen blooms for each stem, depending on how many buds you use in the centre. If you wish to make larger Lantana, then you can have up to four circles of flowers. However, you will end up with a very thick stem.

For added realism roll some green paste, and cut out a very small daisy. If necessary trim the ends of the petals into fine points. Paint a spot of thin royal icing in the middle and push the stem of flowers through the centre and slide the calyx up behind the flowers. Give it time to firm, then use thin green royal icing to paint a calyx on the back, and a little way down the stem to disguise any undue thickness. If you have used green tape and matched the calyx well, your Lantana will be very realistic.

For a much quicker version simply make Basic Blossoms and tape them together. Mixed in a spray with other flowers, these are quite adequate.

Double Blossom

These flowers are pure invention or "fantasy flowers". As such, they can be any colour you choose. They are appropriate for any occasion on a cake. My favourites are white with green centres and red tipped stamens for use on Christmas cakes.

Firstly tape five stamens on to a wire stem. Roll out paste, and cut two pieces for each flower (both the same size). Take the first piece, finger the edges lightly, then flute each petal. Rest on soft foam, and use a ball tool to cup each petal individually, then press firmly in the centre. Next, finger and flute the second set. Place on the foam, and cup each petal. Flip them over, and paint a small dot of egg white in the centre. Position the first set of upward curling petals over the second set of curled-under petals, making sure they alternate. Press firmly in the centre with a ball tool. Take the stem, and using thin royal icing the colour of the flower centre, paint from just above to just below the tape holding the stamens. Push through the centre of the flower until just the stamens, and no tape is showing.

Put aside in a holed board to dry. Once set, paint a calyx on the back using thin green royal icing. To finish, chalk a deeper or contrasting colour in the centre.

Double Blossom are excellent for cascade arrangements.

Browalia

What identifies browalia so easily is the colour combination of brilliant orange and gold flowers, in dense clusters. You really need an airbrush for the best results. If you can achieve the correct colours, then no one will notice if the shapes of the individual flowers aren't quite correct. To this end, I suggest using a five petal blossom cutter if you haven't a specific Browalia cutter.

Colour paste bright yellow, roll thinly, and cut out flowers. Flute round all the petals, and lay face up on soft foam. Press in the centre with a small to medium ball tool, so that the flower dips in the middle, but doesn't actually cup. Insert a bright yellow stamen, and sit in florist foam to set. Once dry, colour royal icing to match, thin slightly with water, and brush it on in a tubular extension on the back of the flower and a little way down the stem. Once dry, spray initially with yellow, then overspray with orange. Try to vary the degree of orange on the flowers, so they are not all the same. Finally, paint a green royal icing calyx on the back. Tape the flowers into clusters before arranging them in sprays.

Buds are made by dipping large stamens further into thin royal icing than normal, then finishing with a calyx in the usual way.

Browalia are ideal for novelty cakes, which often call for very bright colours.

Above: Booties of stiffened tulle cornellied with a fine tube and surrounded by Old World Roses, Basic Blossom and blue Heath to welcome Shani Celeste.

Below: This single tier wedding cake is adorned with a central spray of easy to make Mirabilis. Daisies and Thryptomene are the secondary flowers. The flooded 'bell and bow' lace is very easy to use provided you can handle it by the flooded bell. A matching posy completes the picture.

Five Petal Daisy

Roll out paste thinly and cut out petals (2 sets if you wish to make a double daisy). Finger the edges, then use a pin to press a vein down the centre of each petal. Take care not to go right to the centre of the flower. Place face down on soft foam, and curl the edges by pressing a ball tool from the tip of each petal, in, towards the centre. Turn over and press in the centre. Place on a holed board and insert a piece of wire which has been sprayed or taped, and the tip bent at right angles. Secure with a dot of thin royal icing. For double daisies, make a second set of petals, veined and curled, then placed on top of the first set with a little egg white between. Press firmly in the centre with a ball tool. Once dry, drop a dot of thin royal icing in the centre and sprinkle on some pollen. Shake off any excess and set aside to dry. Once dry, paint a calyx on the back using thin green royal icing.

Try being different by changing the centres. Instead of pollen, tape a number of short stamens to a wire. Paint thin royal icing from just above to just below the stamens, and insert in the centre of the daisy till only the stamens, and no tape shows. Dust some deeper colour chalk along the length of the petals to highlight the veins.

Opposite Page: Godetia are ideal when blue flowers are requested on a cake. In this instance they are teamed with Eriostemon and a few mauve Basic Blossom. Short two inch pillars between the tiers helps achieve a cascade effect.

Cactus Flower

Cactus flowers can be made in bright or pastel colours, or they can be chalked or airbrushed. However you treat them they are a delight on any cake — and so original.

First tape 12 stamens to a wire stem using florists tape. Next roll paste very thin, and cut 2 sets of petals for each flower. Handle the cut shapes carefully as you finger them, then lay face up on soft foam. Use a tool with a rounded point, (such as a short length of knitting needle), and drag along each petal, from the centre out to the edge. Try to avoid marking the very middle of the flower. Treat the second set of petals in the same manner, then paint a touch of egg white in the centre. Lay the first set of petals over the second, so that they are slightly off-set, leaving space for a third row later. Use a medium ball tool, and firmly press in the centre, so that the petals stand up. Place in a holed board. Take the stem of stamens, and use royal icing, coloured to match the centre of the flower, to paint from just above to just below the top of the tape holding the stamens. Insert the stem in the flower, pushing down until only the stamens, and no tape shows. Leave to dry.

Once the flower can be handled, roll more paste very thin and cut another set of petals for each flower. Colour some extra paste green, and use a blossom cutter to make a calyx for each flower. Finger the edges of the calyx, lay on soft foam and paint with egg white. Next work the last set of petals in the same manner as the first two by fingering and pressing down the length of each petal. Place the last set on the calyx, ensuring it attaches properly. Press in the centre with a medium ball tool, and paint with egg white. Take the flower, and insert the stem through the middle of the last round of petals, and slide them up to attach on the back. Make sure they are positioned so they fill the gap left by the first two sets. If your paste is very soft you may find the last petals tend to droop a little. This can be easily overcome by balancing a piece of florist foam between two objects, and suspending the flowers upside-down from the gap between. Once dry paint an extra calyx on the back using thin green royal icing.

The petals of these flowers are joined on by a very narrow neck, and so break off easily. The paste calyx is designed to help strengthen the petals at this weak point, so don't make the calyx too thin, or you will defeat its purpose.

I have tried making all three sets of petals at the same time, but the effect is never as good as doing it in two stages.

If you wish to be a little creative, you can alter the number of stamens, or make them shorter or longer. Try pinching the tips of the petals together for a spikey look.

Frilled Cactus Flower

This flower is made in exactly the same way as the CACTUS FLOWER with one exception. Before pressing down the centre of each petal, gently flute them. They break off easily, so start fluting a little above the narrowest part of the petal. Remember to add a calyx for strength. I have found that these are attractive in shades of mauve with just two rows of petals.

Fruit Blossom

Depending on the colour you choose to make them, these flowers can represent almond, peach, apricot etc. I have used corn silk in the centre, but of course you can use stamens if you prefer.

Line an upturned egg cup with foil, and tape your choice of stamens or corn silk on to a wire stem.

Colour a small amount of paste green (or brown) and cut out the calyx. Finger the edges to thin them, then lay in the foil cup. Roll the petal paste extra thin, and cut five petals for each flower. Finger, chalk, and flute each petal separately. Paint egg white on the calyx, and arrange the petals. Place them between the points of the calyx, and press them firmly so they stick properly. The finished flower should have a fine star of green or brown calyx showing between the petals. Paint a very small amount of thin royal icing from just above to just below the tape holding the stamens, and insert them in the centre of the blossom. Pull through till only stamens, and no tape shows. Set aside to dry. Once dry, remove the foil cups, and if you feel they need extra strength, paint a calyx of royal icing on the back.

Easy Fruit Blossom

Attach ten small stamens to a wire stem using florists tape. Roll paste thinly and cut out flowers. Finger the edges, and chalk on colour if desired. Rest the flower on your index finger and use your fluting tool to roll across the petals from side to side, avoiding the centre of the flower. This should thin the edges further and widen the petals. Place on soft foam, and use a ball tool to curl each petal up and in, by pressing on both corners. Next press in the centre to cup the flower. Take the stamens and using thin royal icing coloured to match the centre of the flower, paint a very thin coat from just above the tape to just below. Push the wire stem through the middle of the flower up to the stamens, so that no tape shows. Place in a holed board to dry — overnight if time permits — before painting a calyx on the back using thin green royal icing. If you are making a large number of these then it is time saving to chalk any colour on once they are finished and dry. You may also like to trim off the stamen tops, and paint some tiny tips on them in your own choice of colour, using very thin royal icing.

See Picture on facing page.

Frangipani

These beautiful flowers have always been popular among cake decorators because they look so lifelike in icing. Most will have learnt to make them fairly soon after taking up sugarcraft. Perhaps all, or part of my technique will help you make even better ones.

Start by packing icing sugar or cornflour into an open container, to a depth of about 4cms (1½ ins). Use an icing nozzle to press a funnel-shaped hole in the cornflour, ready for your first frangipani.

Roll out white paste and cut 5 petals for each flower. Finger the edges of the first petal, and dust yellow chalk to about half way up, blending it in with your thumb. Take your fluting tool and lay it along the left hand edge of the petal (as you look at it, with the pointed end facing towards you). Gently curl the edge of the petal over the tool. This pre-disposes the petal to being rolled up later. Lay it on soft foam and use a marble-size ball tool to slightly cup the rounded end. Make the other 4 petals in the same way, laying them fan-shape on top of

each other, with egg white between. Paint egg white on top of the last petal and roll them up. Make sure the last petal has properly stuck to the back of the first one. Place the flower in the hole made in the cornflour, and use a large soft brush to gently stroke each petal in turn, slowly opening the flower. The cornflour will dry the frangipanis quickly, while holding the petals in place. Buds can be pushed straight into the cornflour, and for tight buds, you can get away with only 3 petals. When they are dry paint a short calyx at the base using thin green royal icing. For realism chalk a touch of pink just a little way up from the calyx. If you need frangipanis on stems, leave the flowers in the cornflour until the petals are almost dry. Because of the thickness at the base you will find it still soft enough to push a wire in amongst the petals. Tape the wire and dip in egg white first. Make sure not to push it too far up into the centre where it will show. Sit in a holed board to dry. Finish with a calyx of thin green royal icing to strengthen and neaten where the wire goes in.

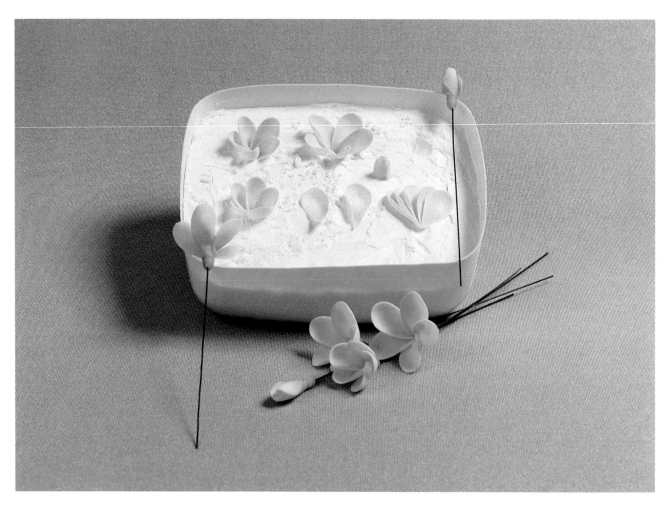

Mirabilis

These flowers normally come in really vibrant pinks and oranges, so I have taken some liberties with colour. They are naturally tubular, but can also be made with a cupped effect. The centres can also be varied by using either pollen or stamens.

WITH STAMENS

Tape 5 stamens on to a stem. Roll icing very thin, and cut out flowers. Finger the edges, then flute generously. Place face up on soft foam and press firmly in the centre with a ball tool. To create a more tubular look press first with a large tool, then a medium, and finally a small ball tool. This way the icing won't split, and the petals will lift and arrange themselves naturally. Paint a fine coat of royal icing (coloured to match the centre of the flower) from just above to just below the tape holding the stamens. Rest the flowers on a holed board, and push the stem through until only the stamens and no tape shows. Allow to set. For a really tubular effect, colour royal icing to match, thin it slightly, and paint on to the back of the flower and a little way down the stem. Once this is dry paint on a green calyx in the normal way. If you wish, the ends of the stamens can be trimmed off, and a touch of very thin royal icing in your choice of colour brushed on the tips. This will give a more delicate look. As a variation, omit the tubular part and simply paint on a green calyx with royal icing.

WITH POLLEN

Roll out icing thinly, and cut out flowers. Finger edges, and flute generously. Place face up on foam and press in centre with medium ball tool so that the petals lift a little. Place on holed board. Take a piece of fine wire which has been taped or sprayed, bend the tip at right angles, and insert in flower. Secure with a tiny drop of royal icing. Once the stems have set, paint a calyx on the back. Allow to dry. At this stage chalk on any desired colours or highlights. Next put a drop of royal icing in the centre, and sprinkle on some pollen. Shake off excess and set aside to dry.

44

Variations

Mirabilis are very versatile. They can be made double, by cutting and working two sets of petals for each flower. Press one set in the centre with the ball tool, then place it on top of the other, with egg white between, and the petals alternated. Press in the centre with a ball tool, and finish either with pollen or stamens and a calyx.

As small filler flowers they are ideal — simply flute, press in the centre with a ball tool so the petals lift and twist, then insert a stamen and finish with a calyx. To look effective the paste must be rolled very thin before cutting out the flowers.

Be creative with your colouring, and try turning some flowers over before you press in the centre with your ball tool.

LEFT: *Cactus Flowers, small Mirabilis, Basic Blossom and Forget-Me-Nots*
CENTRE: *Five Petal Daisies, Daisies, Gypsophila and Forget-Me—Nots.*
RIGHT: *Delicate Open Roses, Fast Open Roses, Double Eriostemon and Pink Boronia.*

Floppy Flower

These are essentially "fantasy flowers", so you can play around with the colour and number of stamens. Firstly tape 5 stamens on to a wire stem. Roll paste very thinly, and cut out flowers. Finger the edges, and flute generously. Place face down on soft foam. Use a tool with a rounded point to gently drag from the middle of the flower, down the centre of each petal to the outside edge. Flip the flower over, and press in the centre with ball tool. Each petal should stand up in the centre with the sides falling away. Colour thin royal icing to match the centre of the flower, and paint it on the stem from just above to just below the tape holding the stamens. Insert in the flower and set to dry in a holed board. Once dry, it can be finished either with a simple royal icing calyx painted on the back, or a tubular extension such as for the fuschia. Finish by chalking a deeper colour in the centre.

Double Floppy Flower

Tape 5 stamens on to a stem and set aside. Roll paste out thinly and cut 2 sets of petals for each flower. Take the first piece, and treat as for single floppy flower. Next take the second piece, finger the edges, and flute generously. Place on soft foam and use a ball tool to cup each petal. Flip the petals over and paint a small spot of egg white in the centre. Place the first set of petals on top, taking care to alternate them, and press in the centre with a ball tool. Colour thin royal icing to match the centre of the flower and paint it on the stem from just above to just below the tape holding the stamens. Insert in the centre of the flower, and set to dry in a holed board. Once set, paint a calyx of thin green royal icing on the back. Place in florist foam to dry. Finally use chalk colours to deepen the centres or perhaps highlight the edges.

Opposite Page: Two rows of lace and an arrangement of bells sets this cake apart. The sprays consist of pink Gumpo Azalias, Eriostemon and mauve Thryptomene.

Lillies

Lillies on a cake are real eyecatchers, provided you reduce them in size a little. As well as white, they come in a host of gay and unusual colours, many with contrasting spots. Most have six petals, in two rows of three, with the top ones being broader than the three underneath. However, if you only have one size cutter, you can still make a very presentable lilly. These instructions apply to making any lilly, regardless of its shape.

You will need a lilly mould (see page 12 for instructions). Prepare the stamens first. You will need seven, with just the tips removed. Tape them on to a stem, with one in the centre for the anther, and six flared around it. Roll tiny pieces of paste, and attach to the stamens with a little egg white (see picture).

Line the lily mould with foil, making it large enough to support the petals till they have dried with the amount of curl you want.

Colour a small amount of paste green, and cut out a calyx. Finger the edges to thin and neaten them, then lay on soft foam, and press in the centre with a ball tool. Fit the calyx into the foil cup.

Roll your petal paste very thin, and cut out six petals. If you have two sizes, work the narrow base petals first. Finger the edges, and dust on any chalk colouring required. Flute the edges just a little, then lay on soft foam. Use the fluting tool to drag along the middle of the petal, from tip to tip. Moisten the calyx with egg white, and arrange the first petal in it. Work the remaining petals in the same way, arranging the last three over, and between the first three. Secure them firmly in place with egg white. Paint thin royal icing, the colour of the flower, from just above to just below the tape holding the stamens. Push the stem down into the centre of the flower till only the stamens, and no tape shows. Set aside to dry.

Depending on the shape of your Lilly, they can provide difficulties if you wish to paint spots on the finished flower. If this is the case, you can get round it by the following method. Omit the calyx, and make the flower as previously described, but without using egg white to stick the petals together. Once dry, remove and spot the petals. Make a calyx, and insert it into the lilly mould. Paint on a thin coat of royal icing, then arrange the petals, taking care to put them back in their original order, and gluing them firmly with thin royal icing. Attach the stamens in the normal way.

Tiger Lillies, Realistic Jasmon, Karume Azalias, and Basic Blossom.

Chrysanthemum

Chrysanthemums are perfect for Mothers day cakes but be cautious when planning to use them on wedding cakes. For many Europeans they represent death.

You will need at least four daisy cutters in graduated sizes. If you wish to make bigger, fuller flowers, then just add extra sizes, and follow the same basic principals. Sit the finished flowers to dry on cotton reels, or small vials or bottles — something that is about the diameter of the smallest set of petals — with a hole through which the wire stem can hang. This allows the outside petals to separate and hang down, and the flower finishes up with a rounded, rather than flat appearance.

TYPE A

To keep the flower from looking chunky, roll the paste very thin, and cut two sets of each size petals. Start with the largest ones. Lay the petals on your index finger, and use a fluting tool to roll along the length of the petal, from the centre out. This will help make the edges very fine. Lay on soft foam, and use your fluting tool to drag the

length of the petal, again, from the centre out. Turn over, and put a tiny speck of egg white in the centre. Work all but the last three sets of petals in the same way, and in decreasing order of size. Lay them on top of one another as you go, alternating the petals, and with a

tiny bit of egg white between. Roll the third last set of petals with the fluting tool, lay on the foam, and use a ball tool to slightly curl the tips upwards. Place in the centre of the flower. Treat the last two sets in the same manner, only curling them a little more before putting them in place. Roll out some more icing, and cut one extra row of large petals, and work them in the same manner as the first. Put a little egg white in the centre, and place the flower on top of them, then press firmly in the middle with a ball tool, so that the smallest petals in the middle curl right over. Lift the flower by using tweezers as a prong, and sit it on a bottle to dry. The last row of petals, being fresher, therefore softer, should fall back nicely. Use the tweezers to coax individual petals into position.

B

A

C

From Page 50.

Cover a short length of wire with tape, bend the tip at right angles, and insert in the centre of the flower. Secure with a tiny spot of royal icing. When the flowers are dry, paint a calyx on the back using thin green royal icing, and sit in florists foam to dry. Finally, finish the flowers by dropping a dot of royal icing in the centre, sprinkle on some pollen, and shake off any excess.

TYPE B

Roll your paste very thin, and cut out two sets of each size petal. Starting with the largest set, lay them on your index finger, and use a fluting tool to roll the length of the petal, from the middle out to the ends. Lay on soft foam, and use the fluting tool to drag down the centre of each petal, again, from the centre out to the tips. Put a tiny spot of egg white in the middle, and put aside. Work all but the remaining two rows in the same way, adding them to the first, with egg white between, and alternating the petals. Roll the second last set with the fluting tool, then use a ball tool to curl the petals up, before placing them in the middle of the flower. Repeat for the last set.

Roll out some more paste, and cut an extra set of large petals. Treat them as for the first set, put a spot of egg white in the centre, then use your tweezers as flat prongs to lift the flower on to them. Finally, press firmly in the centre with a ball tool to cup the two smallest rows. Use the tweezers to lift the flower, and sit it on a small bottle to dry. Make sure the petals separate and fall back a little. Insert a stem, and finish off in the same manner as described for type A.

TYPE C

Roll the icing very thin, and cut two sets of each size petals. Start with the largest ones. Lay them on your index finger, and use a fluting tool to roll along the length of each petal, from the centre out. Lay on soft foam, and use a ball tool to curl the tip of each petal, by pressing and pulling towards the centre. Paint a speck of egg white in the middle, and put to one side. Work the remaining petals in the same way, in decreasing order of size. Curl each set a little more than the last, before arranging them on top of one another. Use egg white between the layers, and take care to alternate the petals.

Roll out some more paste, and cut out another large set of petals. Work them in the same manner as the first. Paint a little egg white in the middle of them, then use your tweezers as prongs to lift the flower and place it on top. Finally press firmly in the centre with a ball tool. Use your tweezers to lift the flower on to a small jar to dry. Make sure the petals separate and fall back a little. Insert a stem, and finish off in the same manner as described for type A.

CALYX

Once the Chrysanthemum is dry, roll some paste into a small ball. Push the flower stem through the ball and slide it up to the back of the flower and attach with some egg white. Roll some green past very thin, and cut two sets of the smallest size petals for each calyx. Finger the edges, then lay on soft foam. Place one on top of the other, alternating the petals, and with egg white between. Select a ball tool which matches the size of the ball of icing you have already stuck to the flower, and press the centre of the calyx. Paint with egg white and slide up to cover the paste ball and flare on to the back of the flower itself.

BUDS

Simply cut out three or four of the smallest size sets of petals. Finger the edges, lay on soft foam, and use a ball tool to slightly curl the tip of each petal. Lay the sets on top of each other, alternating the petals and with a touch of egg white between. Press firmly in the centre with a fairly large ball tool so that the petals stand up. Tape a piece of wire, bend the end at right angles and insert in the bud, securing it with a small amount of Royal Icing. Sit in a holed board and gently push the petals into the centre of the flower, so it has a full appearance and the wire can't be seen. Once dry finish with a calyx in the same manner as for the main flower, only omit the small ball of paste.

Orchids, Basic Jasmin and Crowea.

Godetia

Godetia are one of the few icing flowers that look natural in blue, so they are a handy flower to have in your repertoire.

Cut 10 to 15 small stamens to about 1/3 their length (save the pieces left in the middle to make crowea). Tape the stamens on to a short length of fine wire using florist's tape. Spread them slightly to give a natural effect. Take a small piece of foil to line the upturned base of an egg cup, or anything that will form a small cup shape.

Cut a pale green calyx, not too thin, and use a fluting tool to roll from about half way down the petal out to the edge, thinning it nicely. Press the calyx into the centre of the foil. Roll white paste thinly and cut four petals for each flower. Lightly finger them and dust the edges with colour. Flute generously, then place face up on soft foam and press a large ball tool on the bottom half (pointed end) of the petal, to slightly cup it.

Paint the calyx with egg white, and place a dot of thin royal icing in the centre. Arrange the petals in the calyx, painting each one with egg white where it overlaps the previous one. Tuck the last petal under the first. Paint a thin coat of royal icing, coloured to match the centre of the flower, from just above, to just below the tape holding the stamens. Push the stem gently through the centre of the Godetia, until only the stamens show and none of the tape. If necessary, use thin royal icing to paint around the stamens and neaten the centre. Sit on a holed board to dry. If you haven't a hole in your egg cup, then you will need to lift the alfoil and flower up to insert the stamens.

Opposite Page: This cream cake is for the modern Bride who wants it to be a talking point at the reception. The cakes are three differnt shapes, and the cream lace pillars are two different heights and widths. The sprays consist of Fast Open Roses with cornsilk stamens, Miniature Orchids, and cream Heath.

Azalia

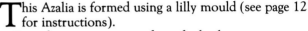

This Azalia is formed using a lilly mould (see page 12 for instructions).

Tape 6 stamens, ranging from fairly short, to very long, on to a wire stem using florists tape.

Use the lilly mould to form a foil cup for each flower. Colour a small amount of paste green, roll thinly, and cut a calyx for each flower. Use a fluting tool to roll from side to side on each point, broadening them and thinning the edges at the same time. Place on soft foam and press firmly in the centre with a medium ball tool. Fit the calyx into the foil cup, making sure the points are evenly arranged.

Roll the petal paste very thin, and cut 6 petals for each flower. Finger the edges of the first petal, and flute. Lay face up on soft foam, and use a tool with a softly rounded point (such as a short piece of knitting needle) to drag along the centre length of the petal. Paint the calyx with egg white, and position the first petal. Make sure the petal goes right down to the centre of the calyx and is firmly attached. Gently curl the top of the petal back. The edges should stand up slightly. Finish another two petals in the same way, and position them evenly in the calyx. Work the three remaining petals, paint egg white on their backs, and lay them on top of, and between, the first three. Curl the petals back slightly.

Paint thin royal icing, coloured to match the centre of the flower, on the stem from just above to just below the tape holding the stamens. Insert in the centre of the azalia, pulling down till only the stamens and no tape shows. If you haven't made a hole in your mould, lift the foil cup out to insert the stem. Stand in a holed board to dry. Once dry, chalk a touch of colour on the tip of each petal, and a little deeper colour in the centre if required.

These azalias are not suitable for cascade arrangements, they are at their best in more formal sprays.

Karume Azalia

These small azalias can be made in a host of pretty colours, and are perfect for wedding cakes.

Tape six stamens of differing lengths on to a short stem of wire. Ideally the stamens should be the same colour as the flower. Use a Karume Azalia Mould (see page 12 for instructions) to make foil cups to form the flowers in.

Roll paste very thin, and cut two pieces for each flower. Finger the edges of the first set, and flute just the very edges all the way round. These petals break off easily, so you will need to treat them carefully. Place face up on soft foam, and press with a ball tool. To achieve a tubular look, press first with a large, then a medium, and finally a small ball tool. With this method the centre is stretched gradually, and avoids tearing. Sit the petals in the foil cup using a small ball tool to press it well down. Fold the petals back, and paint the centre with egg white.

Finger and flute just the edges of the second set of petals. Lay face down on soft foam, and use a tool with a softly rounded point to drag along the backs of the petals, from the middle out to the tips, avoiding the very centre of the flower. Turn the flower over, and press in the centre as for the first set. Lay the second set over the first, ensuring the petals alternate and stand up a little. Press the centre with a small ball tool so the two pieces stick together.

Paint thin royal icing, coloured to match the centre of the flower, on to the stem from just above to just below the tape holding the stamens. Insert in the centre of the azalia, and pull through until only the stamens, and no tape shows. Sit in a holed board until it is firm enough to handle, but not completely dry. Paint speckles in a deeper shade on one petal, and few spots on the petals either side. By painting the speckles on before the flower is completely dry they will have a softer look, and dry faster.

Once the flower has dried, paint a small calyx on the back, using thin green, or brown royal icing.

Tape the flowers together in twos and threes before arranging.

Opposite & Below: Soft pink Karume Azalias, Daisies, and a scaterring of mauve Thryptomene combine in this modern arrangement of cakes. The heart shaped box on top was made from a chocolate mould.

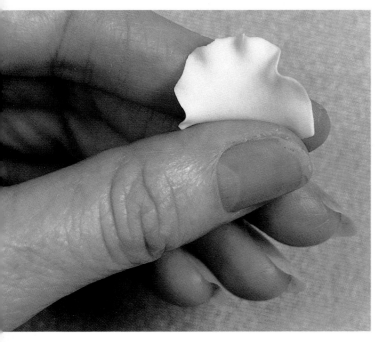

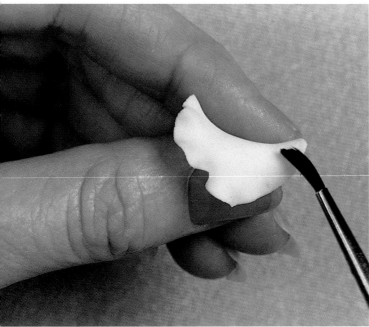

Gumpo Azalia

Gumpo Azalias are naturally white, with yellow centres, however I make them whatever colour a client requests, including bright red for Christmas cakes. They are most effective if the stamen stalks are the same colour as the flower centre. If you can't find the all-colour ones in shops, it is a simple matter to colour white stamen stalks with chalk, after they have been taped on to wire stems. If you have an air brush, it is even easier to spray them.

You will need an azalia mould to make these flowers (see page 12 for instructions).

Tape five stamens on to a wire stem using florists tape. If the stalks are white, spray or chalk them to match the colour you have chosen for the centres of the flowers.

Use the azalia mould to form a foil cup for each flower. Colour a small amount of paste green, roll out, and cut a calyx for each flower. Use a fluting tool to roll along each point, from the centre out, thinning the edges. Lay on soft foam and press in the centre with a ball tool. Sit the calyx in the foil cup and paint with egg white.

Roll petal paste very thin, and cut five petals for each flower. Finger the edges, and chalk colour on to the base. Flute generously all the way round. At this stage the petal should be held between the thumb and forefinger, with the rounded edge towards your palm, and the chalked side facing you. Fold down the centre, by bringing half the petal forward over your thumb. Use your other hand to gently curve the pointed end backwards. Paint a little egg white on the pointed corner facing you. Lay the petal on its side in the calyx, pressing the part with egg white firmly into the calyx, and leaving the other half standing away from it, to fill the centre of the flower. Treat the remaining petals in the same manner, adding them to the calyx as they are made, overlapping them, and working in a clockwise direction. Tuck the last petal under the first. Use the five peaks of the calyx as an indicator for positioning the petals, and make sure the point of each petal goes well down into the centre of the calyx.

Take the stem, and using thin royal icing, coloured to match the centre of the flower, paint from just above to just below the tape holding the stamens. Insert in the centre of the Azalia, pulling through until only the stamens, and no tape shows. If you haven't made a hole in your azalia mould, you will need to lift the foil cup out to do this. Set aside on a holed board to dry.

Because they are fairly flat flowers, Gumpo Azalias are useful for cascade arrangements, and are suitable for bell cakes.

The tiers on this cake are all set level at the back, leaving room at the front for large sprays of apricot Miniature Open Roses, Eriostemon and mauve Heath. Two gold rings and a pair of doves add a romantic touch.

Fuschia

Fuschias need to be hanging to look effective — They tend to lose their impact when all laying face up on a cake. Try to have at least one or two hanging over the side, so they are shown to their best advantage. Lay some flowers on their sides to dry, so the sepals will flatten slightly as they would if you were to lay a fresh flower down. They will be easier to arrange and less inclined to break.

Firstly tape eight short and one long stamen on to a wire stem. The stamens should rightly be the same colour as the sepal.

Roll the petal paste thinly and cut one set for each flower. Rest the petals on your index finger, and use a fluting tool to roll from side to side across each alternate petal. Turn them over and roll the remaining petals. Lay on soft foam, and press in the centre with a ball tool. Paint the centre with egg white then insert the stem through the middle and push the petals up to just short of the stamens. Carefully fold the petals round the stamen, then stand in a holed board and allow to firm a little before proceeding. Once the first petals have partly dried, roll out more petal paste, and cut a second set for each flower, working them as before. Paint the middle with egg white, insert the stem through the centre, and push this second set of petals up and attach to the first, folding them in gently. The petals should be evenly gathered round the stamens, with some petals curved inwards, and some outwards. Make sure the two sets have stuck together before setting in a holed board to dry. When dry, chalk on any extra colour required before proceeding with the sepal.

Once the centres are dry, roll out the sepal paste, and cut one piece for each flower. Carefully finger the edges, then lay on soft foam. Use a ball tool to curl each point, starting at the very tip and pulling towards the centre. Flip the sepal over, and press in the centre. Paint the middle with egg white, insert the stem through the centre of the sepal, then push up and attach to the underside of the flower. Press firmly to ensure it is attached properly. Colour some royal icing to match the sepal, and thin it slightly with water. Use a brush to paint the royal icing on to the back of the sepal and a little way down the stem to create a tubular effect. Once this has set, finish off with a small calyx painted in thin green royal icing at the sepal's base. Sit the flower in florists foam to dry.

To finish, paint the front and back of the sepals with egg white, so that once dry it will have a waxy look to match the part made with royal icing.

Fuschia Bud

Tape a few short stamens on to a wire stem. Roll the sepal icing thinly and cut out. Finger the edges gently, and lay on soft foam. Use a fairly large ball tool to curl each petal, starting from the tip, and pulling towards the centre. Paint the middle with a small amount of thin royal icing, and insert the stem. Push the bud up the stem till the tips of the stamens will just peep through when the bud is closed around them. To help them hold their shape while drying, hang them upside down from a piece of florists' foam balanced between two objects. When dry, paint with egg white for a waxy look, and add a small calyx using thin green royal icing.

Gold Miniature Formal Roses, Double Eriostemon, mauve Gypsophila and a few tiny Forget-Me-Nots decorate this Golden Anniversary Cake.

Congratulations Florence and Peter 50 yrs

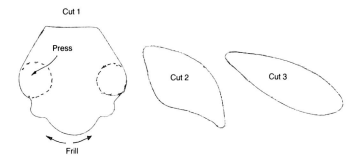

Cymbidium Orchid

The popularity of orchids has never waned, probably because they add a touch of glamour to cakes. This method is really easy to master so give it a try — you may surprise yourself.

Most orchid cutters are made with the lip coming to a point at the back. For this method simply cut out as normal, then trim off the extra part, so that when the lip is shaped, the back will be flat, and rest easily against the petals.

Firstly form the tongue using moulding paste. The size depends on the cutters you are using, so you may have to experiment at first. Tape a short length of wire, dip in egg white, and insert it in the tongue. Don't push it all the way up, about half way is sufficient. Lay the tongue on soft foam and press the tip with a ball tool, so that it will have a slight downward curl when attached to the lip. Allow these to at least partially dry, then chalk a little colour on the tip. Next roll the icing thinly and cut out the lip. Finger the edges, and chalk on colour, blending it in with your thumb. Flute generously round the edges, then lay face up on soft foam. Press on both edges with a fairly large ball tool (where indicated in the diagram). Paint egg white on the sides and top of the tongue, avoiding the chalked tip, then wrap the lip around it. The sides of the lip should meet at the stem end, and be slightly apart at the front. Use sharp scissors to trim the area around the wire, by cutting away any excess icing from the lip or tongue. It should be nice and flat so it will sit straight up from the petals. Stand the stem in florist foam to dry. If you wish to paint spots on the lip, do so before it is completely dry, as it will produce a soft velvety look, and more natural appearance.

The next step is to press some aluminium foil into shapes to hold the finished flowers. I use a patty-pan tray for this, and have drilled a hole in the centre of each cup to allow the stem through. (The flowers can be left to dry in the container this way) However, cardboard fruit trays are just as good, if not as permanent. For very small orchids, the upturned base of an egg cup is ideal.

When the lips are dry, roll some more paste thinly, and cut out 3 back petals and 2 side petals for each flower. Begin with the back petals. Finger the edges and dust on any colouring. Lay on soft foam and use a large ball tool to gently drag the length of the petal. Start from the outside tip, and pull towards the centre, so that the petal is curved both ways. Arrange them in the alfoil, the top one first, then the bottom two, overlapping them in the centre and using egg white between each one. Finger the side petals, chalk on any colour, and flute them as little, or as much as you want. Position side petals on top of the base petals, overlapping them and painting egg white between.

Take the lip, and using thin royal icing coloured to match the centre of the orchid, paint the area at the back of the lip around the wire stem. Insert the wire through the centre of the petals, and push the lip down firmly so it grips onto the petals without actually tearing them. Use a small paint brush to smooth over any excess royal icing, and help camouflage the join. If necessary, prop the lip in place with cotton balls, taking care they don't stick to the royal icing.

Long after the petals have dried, the centre will still be soft because it has five layers of paste in it. Therefore you should allow at least 24 hours drying time. Store the finished orchids in their foil cups to avoid breakages.

Real orchids have a waxy look about them, which with extra time and patience you can copy. Make the orchids in the usual way, but avoid using chalks for colouring. Any highlights should be applied using food colouring, either mixed into the paste, or airbrushed or painted on before the paste has dried.

Once the flower is finished, and has been allowed to dry properly, use a large soft brush to paint on a thin coat of egg white. Take care not to apply too much, and avoid leaving little bubbles all over the flowers. Again allow to dry, after which you can dust on a little chalk for highlights — not too much or you will spoil the waxy look.

Miniature Orchid

Miniature orchids look beautiful with open roses, and can be made to suit any colour scheme. They trail easily and are useful for cascade arrangements.

Most orchid cutters are made with the lip coming to a point at the back. For this method, simply cut out as normal, then trim off the extra part, so that when the lip is shaped, the back will be flat, and rest neatly against the petals.

If you want the finished flowers on strong stems, tape some fine wire, and use egg white to attach a small tongue of paste to one end. Occasionally I have had stamens with heads that are big enough to use as tongues, but if none are available, paint a little extra royal icing on a stamen until it is the right size to suit your orchid's lip. Allow to dry.

Roll paste thinly, and cut out lip. Finger the edges, and flute the front of the lip. As it is so small, a fine fluting tool, and plenty of practice will help. Paint egg white on the tongue, and wrap the lip around it. The two sides should touch at the stem end, and be a little apart at the front. Sit in florists foam to dry. If you want to paint spots on the tongue, they are best done before it is completely dry, to give a soft velvety look. Once they are dry, roll some more paste thinly, and cut one set of Jasmin petals for each lip. Use a fluting tool, and roll it from side to side on each petal, avoiding the centre and thinning the edges. Place them face down on soft foam, and use a ball tool to stroke and slightly curl both upper side petals. Leave the other three as they are. Flip the petals over. Take the lip, and paint a small amount of thin royal icing, coloured to match the flower, on the back where the wire or stamen goes into the lip. Push the stem through the centre of the petals, and position the lip correctly. Use a small brush to smooth any excess icing around the lip, and camouflage the join. Set in a holed board to dry, then finish with a calyx using thin green royal icing, and chalk on any colours you fancy.

Miniature orchids can be varied by reversing the treatment of the petals. Curl the top petal, and lower side petals forward, and they will look slightly smaller and noticeably different.

Roses

Old World Rose

When I first saw this beautiful little rose in a florist shop I thought Mother Nature must have had cake decorators in mind when she made them. They were so simple to copy, and so lifelike when finished, that I knew they were a "must" for this book.

Firstly tape cornsilk on to a stem. (See page 12). Cut the silk straight across, so the pieces are all the same length, then tip a brush in caramel or light brown liquid food colouring and lightly pass it across the tips of the silk. Spread the silk stamens out, and set aside to dry.

Colour some paste green, and cut a calyx for each flower — keep the colour pale, or it will show through the finished flower. Lay the calyx over your index finger, and use a fluting tool to roll along the stems, from the middle, out to the tips.

Roll the flower paste very thin, and cut out one piece for each flower. Finger the edges, and dust the outsides with pink chalk. Use a fine fluting tool, and work round all the petals, so they lift a little, rather than actually frill. Paint egg white on the calyx, and place the rose on top. Make the points of the calyx correspond with the petals, so they give them strength, otherwise they break off very easily. Make sure they are stuck together, then press in the centre with a ball tool. This is not meant to cup the flower, but to lift and twist the petals. The finished flowers should have a rather flat appearance. Paint thin royal icing on the stem just below the stamens, and insert it in the centre of the rose. Sit in a holed board to dry. As old world roses mature the petals tend to arch backwards, so stand a few flowers in foam to dry, and if necessary, gently ease the petals back a little.

Once dry, colour some thin royal icing to match the calyx, and paint a little "hip" on each flower. Stand in florist foam to dry. If you prefer, they can be made all white, and colour chalked on afterwards.

Buds are made in the same way, but cupped using a fairly large ball tool.

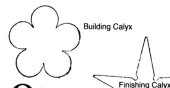

Building Calyx

Finishing Calyx

Open Roses

There is basically only one way of making open roses, however, by using different numbers of petals, cutters, and centres, you can produce any number of different flowers. They are all attractive, but some are quicker to make than others, and I tend to use them more often.

CALYX There are special rose calyx cutters available, but a blossom cutter makes a better base to BUILD your flower on. if the back of the rose will be showing in the finished arrangement, then a fancy calyx is added last. Bear in mind that the roses are harder to arrange if you have the petals of the calyx curling back. Either way, the calyx you build your rose on won't show, so it is a great time saver to use the same clour paste as the petals.

FINISHING CALYX Roll dark green paste thinly, and cut out calyx. Finger the edges, and lay on soft foam. Use a ball tool to curl each point, dragging from the very tip, in, toward the centre. Turn the calyx over, and press in the centre. Paint the middle and a little way down each point with egg white. Push the rose stem through the middle of the calyx, slide it up, and attach to the underside of the rose. Press it on firmly, and curl the calyx points down nicely, but take care to hide the original calyx. You can finish it off nicely by colouring some royal icing to match the calyx, thinning it slightly and painting a small "hip" under it.

CENTRES You can also finish your roses in one of four ways.
A . . . Pipe a ball of royal icing in the centre, sprinkle on some pollen, and shake off any excess.
B . . . Pipe a ball of royal icing in the centre, sprinkle on some pollen, shake off any excess, then surround it with curved stamens. Curl them first, and tuck them under the icing centre.
C . . . Tape as many stamens as you can handle on to a stem, paint thin royal icing from just above to just below the tape, and insert in the centre of the rose till only the stamens, and no tape shows.
D . . . Use a cornsilk centre as described on page 12.

Delicate Open Rose

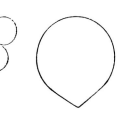

Start by making a foil cup to form the roses in. The size depends on how big you intend making your roses. I suggest lining a patty-pan tin or fruit tray for large roses, and an upturned egg cup is ideal for small roses.

Roll paste and cut out calyx. Use a fluting tool to roll the petals from the centre outwards, thinning the edges. Press the calyx into the centre of the foil cup. Roll petal paste very thin (almost transparent), and cut out six petals. Finger the edges, and chalk on any colour you require, blending it in with your thumb. Flute the edges generously. Work all the petals in the same way. Paint the calyx with egg white, then arrange the petals in it. The points should not quite meet in the centre, and the petals should overlap, with the last one tucked under the first. Make sure each petal has been pressed on to the calyx. Roll another lot of paste very thin, and use the same cutter to make five more petals. Work them in the same manner, before arranging in the centre of the first petals. Paint egg white on the backs of the petals where they overlap, and tuck the last one under the first. Only the point of the petals should be pushed on to the calyx, so the petals stand up, and fill the centre of the flower. If necessary support the petals with tiny pieces of cotton wool. I usually finish these roses with a stem of stamens, but they look attractive with just pollen centres, or pollen and stamens together. If you have rolled the paste very thin, these flowers are almost weightless when finished, and are ideal for use in bouquets and corsages. They also trail nicely for cascade arrangements.

Basic Dog Rose

Start by making a foil cup to form the roses in. The size of the cup will depend on how big you intend making your roses. I use patty-pan tins for large and average flowers, and upturned egg cups for small onces.

Roll paste and cut out a calyx. Use a fluting tool to roll the petals from the centre, out to the edge, thinning them nicely. Place the calyx in the centre of the foil cup, and paint with egg white. Roll out the petal paste, and cut five petals for each flower. Finger the edges, and brush on any chalk colouring required, blending it in with your thumb. Flute the edges, then lay on soft foam. Use a large ball tool to press in the centre, cupping the petal, as well as accentuating the fluting. Work the other petals in the same manner. Arrange the petals on the calyx, overlapping each petal, and having all the points meeting in the centre. Brush egg white on the backs of the petals where they overlap, and tuck the last petal under the first. Flowers are easier to arrange if they have stems, and open roses are no exception. If you are not using method C or D for your centre, then proceed as follows:—

Tape a short length of wire, bend the tip at right angles, and insert in the centre of the rose. Secure with a tiny drop of royal icing. Once dry finish the centre using either method A or B.

Double Dog Rose

Proceed as for BASIC DOG ROSE, except when placing the first set of petals in the calyx, position them so that the points don't quite meet in the centre. Cut out a second set of slightly smaller petals, and finger, chalk, and flute them in the same way. Lay on soft foam and press in the centre with a large ball tool. Arrange these petals over the first, taking care to alternate them. Paint the backs with egg white, and have all the petals meeting in the centre. Finish with whatever centre method you choose. You may find it necessary to support the centre petals with small pieces of rolled cotton wool until they dry.

Opposite Page: What could be more romantic than pale pink Miniature Formal Roses, Eriostemon and mauve Coral Flowers, set against white pillars, with Lily of the Valley embroidery, lace and extension. Small white doves add the finishing touch.

68

Fast Open Rose

This rose is made in exactly the same way as the DELICATE OPEN ROSE, except I use a heart shaped cutter, and only four petals on the outside and three on the inside. Both sets of petals are the same size.

Because they are the product of a need to have finished flowers in a hurry, I give them pollen centres. (method A). They have become popular with my customers, who usually pick them over the fancier ones. It may take practice to produce nice ones, but once you have mastered them, they are extremely handy to know, and so quick to make.

Miniature Open Rose

These little roses come in a multitude of glorious colours, so experiment to find out the tones you like best in them. They sound complicated to make, but are not really, and for the finished size and appearance, are quite fast to make. I have shown the cutter sizes I use for medium roses but they can be made bigger or smaller.

Roll paste very thin (almost transparent), and cut out one small, and two large sets of petals for each flower. Work the smaller set first. Finger the edges and flute each petal generously. Use sharp scissors, or a scalpel to cut between each petal — not too far or they will tear off as you work them. Place on soft foam and use a ball tool to cup each petal, then press in the centre. Because of the cuts you made, the petals should tend to overlap. Set these aside, then finger and flute the first set of large petals. Place on soft foam, cup each petal with a ball tool, then slightly cup the centre as well. Finger and flute the third set of petals, lay on the foam, and slightly cup each petal only. Paint a spot of egg white in the centre, and lay the second set of petals on them, making sure they alternate. Paint a touch of egg white in the centre, and add the small set of petals,

again alternating them.

Press very firmly in the centre, so that the centre petals almost close over. Tape a short length of wire, bend the tip at right angles, and insert it through the centre of the rose, securing with a spot of thin royal icing. Set in a holed board to dry.

When they are dry enough to handle, roll out another lot of paste very thinly, and cut out one set of large petals for each flower. Finger them lightly, then flute round the edges. Lay on soft foam, and cup each petal. Flip the petals over, and paint egg white in the middle area. Push the rose stem through the centre, and slide the last lot of petals up to the back of the rose. Alternate them before pressing into place. Sit in florist foam, and allow the last set of downward curled petals to settle naturally. Once dry, paint a drop of thin royal icing in the centre, sprinkle on some pollen, and shake off any excess. Finish simply with a calyx of thin green royal icing, or by the following method:—

Roll green paste thinly and use a Jasmin cutter to cut out a calyx for each flower. Finger the edges, and lay on soft foam. Use a ball tool to curl each petal by dragging from the tip, in towards the centre. Flip over, and press firmly in the centre. Moisten about half way along each point with egg white, insert the rose stem through the centre, and push the calyx up the stem. Fasten the calyx to the rose about half way along each point, so the centre where you pressed the ball tool hangs down to represent the hip. It's not necessary, but I finish with a small spot of thin green royal icing at the base of the calyx.

BUDS

Tape a short length of wire, dip the end in egg white, and attach a tiny moulded bud. Set aside to dry. Roll paste very thin and cut one set of petals for each bud. Finger the edges, and flute all the way round. Cut two of the petals away (where indicated in the diagram), and press in the centre of both with a ball tool. Moisten the bud with egg white and wrap the two petals tightly around it. Use sharp scissors or a scalpel to nick between the remaining three petals. Press in the centre of each petal with a ball tool, turn over, moisten with egg white, and wrap around the bud, allowing them to flair a little at the top. Finish with a calyx as for the full flower.

Miniature Formal Rose

At first glance, making these flowers would seem to be a long job — they do need time to dry between each stage. However, if you are making several, by the time you finish stage one of the last flower, you can usually start on stage two of the first flower, and so on down the line.

Firstly tape some wire stems and form a small paste bud on each. Allow to dry.

When the buds have dried, roll the petal paste very thin, and stamp out one set for each flower. Cut off two petals (where indicated on the pattern above), and if they are not very well defined petals, cut a little way in between each petal. Finger and flute the piece with two petals, and lay on soft foam. Press in the centre of each with a ball tool to cup, then paint them both amply with egg white. Fold the petals round the bud, taking care to cover it completely, and press on firmly. Finger and flute the remaining piece, again cutting in a little way between the petals. Lay on soft foam, and cup each petal slightly with a ball tool, turn over, paint with egg white, and wrap around the bud, again taking care to see they stick well to the first set. Fold the very tips of the petals back a little. Trim of any excess icing at the base with a scalpel or scissors, and set aside to at least partly dry.

Roll out more paste and cut another set for each flower. Finger the edges and as before, cut a little way in between each petal. Flute well, lay on soft foam, and cup each petal slightly, then press in the centre. Colour a little thin royal icing to match the flower, and paint it sparingly round the base of the bud, before inserting the stem into the centre of the petals, and pushing them up to attach to the bud. The royal icing will run in and fill any gaps. Leave the flowers to set slightly either in a holed board, or hanging upside down in florists foam suspended between two objects. Roll some more icing, finger the edges, slit between the petals, and flute generously. Lay on soft foam, and press only in the centre with a ball tool. Paint the middle with either a small amount of thin royal icing or egg white, then push the stem through, and attach the petals firmly to the back of the flower. Stand in florists foam to dry, so the petals can drop back a little. To finish, paint a calyx on the back using thin green royal icing, and highlight the centre with a deeper colour chalk.

If you wish, you can make a calyx for the back using a jasmin cutter as for the Miniature Open Rose.

Ribbon Loops

The shine of fine ribbon loops, peeping from between paste flowers not only adds life, and an extra dimension to arrangements, but can serve to hide stems, and hold flowers in place. Make the loops of varying heights, and put them in place first, where the main body of the spray will be. Arrange your feature flowers over and amongst the loops, then add the secondary and filler flowers. You will find you need fewer small flowers, and the loops will keep them in place — the stems need only be pushed a little way into the covering icing. In damp weather, when paste flowers would normally sag, the ribbon will hold them up. If you wish the ribbon loops to be unobtrusive, make them the same colour as the cake. If they are to be a feature, then use coloured loops, but take care that they don't overpower the flowers, which should always be the focus of attention.

By arranging the loops first, you can avoid breakages, because you simply follow the line they create, and you should not need to be shifting flowers around. This method makes arranging posies especially easy.

For safety reasons, loops should always be constructed so that when they are pulled out of the cake, there is no chance of the wire being left behind. The simplest method is to form the ribbon into figure of eights, holding them in the middle. Bend a short length of wire across the centre and down. Hold the wire tightly and twist the loops to make them stand up. If you are making a lot of loops, I advise using the rayon covered wire. Apart from being easier to use, it keeps your fingers from becoming very tender.

If you are taping flowers into corsages, remember that the base of the ribbon loops must go right down to the holding point. In wired arrangements, the loops are meant to hide the mechanics, as well as enhance the flowers. Short loops on a long length of wire will do neither. With this in mind, make the loops as you need them, and check to see how long they need to be to do both jobs satisfactorily.

Should the need arise, you can even use ribbon loops to deceive the eye into seeing what basically isn't there. For instance, Frangipani's, with yellow loops, will make a yellow spray. With pink loops, and a sprinkling of small pink flowers, you can have a pink arrangement, even though you used basically yellow flowers.

Miriabilis, Eriostemon and sprigs of Basic Blossom

Frangipanis, Eriostemon and Heath.

Leaves

Most arrangements are enhanced by leaves, provided they are well made and suitably proportioned. From a floristy point of view it is not necessary to match the flowers with their natural leaves. Both the colour and shape can either harmonise with the flowers for a soft look, or be a contrasting feature. If you make all your leaves pale green they can be airbrushed or touched up with chalk to make them darker for contrast, or left pale, and highlighted with soft colours to harmonise with your arrangements.

Use either a plastic leaf as a mould, or pick a fresh leaf from the garden.

Roll your paste thinly and cut out the leaves. Lay them on the mould, and press firmly to transfer the pattern of the veins on to the paste. Press as hard as possible round the edges, so they will be extremely fine — many a beautiful spray has been spoilt by thick leaves. Twist or curl some of the leaves before setting them to dry, and they will add movement to your finished arrangements.

Above: Fine leaves airbrushed in Autumn colours, ribbon and berries (buds) make for an easy male 21st cake.

Twist or curl some leaves before setting to dry, and they will add movement to your finished arrangements.

74

Arrangements

The very best advice I can offer is to try and attend floristry lessons. Failing that, here are a few basic rules you can apply towards decorating cakes with flowers.

Before starting, always have in your mind the line you wish the finished spray to take, and stick to it. Keep the deepest flowers in the centre, and avoid putting dark, or eyecatching colours at the outermost points, unless they are very small. If you can visualise a triangle (not necessarily an even one), and keep your arrangement within its boundaries, you will be on the right track. The biggest and/or best flowers should be the focal point, and the rest of the flowers serve only to draw your eyes toward it. Create depth by having flowers at differing heights. In a good, well balanced arrangement, all the flowers should appear to come from the one central point, so tilt the flowers as you place them. Try to avoid crowding — each flower should be able to "speak for itself".

The modern trend in arranging flowers places the emphasis on style, rather than the number of flowers. A simple, uncluttered spray will look far more professional than one which is heavy, over crowded, or "busy". Make your golden rule "When in doubt, leave it out".

Double Blossom, Tubular Eriostemon, and Forget-Me-Nots.

75

Instruction for Tulle Bell

The tulle bell featured on some of the wedding cakes pictured is very easily made, however you will need a large plastic or metal bell as a mould.

Cut a small piece of COTTON tulle (not nylon) to roughly fit round the bell. As all bell moulds are different, it is impossible to supply a pattern, but you should end up with a piece approximately the shape of a third of a circle. Allow for shrinkage. Lightly grease the mould, using something which will not discolour the tulle (copha is ideal). Dip the tulle in stiffener (recipe page 80), blot off any excess, and wrap it round the bell. Make sure it is nice and tight, and simply overlap for a join. Trim off any extra at the top, and make several little downward cuts. Fold these small pieces over one another to neatly finish the top. Any overhang at the bottom can be tucked under. Leave to dry before trimming round the base. A little warmth to melt the grease is all that is needed to enable you to twist the dried tulle shape off the mould. Use a fine tube (00) to cornelli over the bell. Once finished, it is almost impossible to detect the join down the side. It doesn't show in the photos, but I have finished the bells with a pretty bow on the top.

Edible Shine for Leaves

EDIBLE SHINE FOR LEAVES

A   1 part Gum Arabic (Acacia Gum)
     3 parts water

Put water in a small bowl or cup and sprinkle with the Gum Arabic. Stand in a pot of water and boil until the gum has dissolved. To use, keep on a gentle boil, and take the leaves to the stove. The mix dries very quickly, so you must work deftly and fairly fast. Use a brush wide enough to cover the leaves so they are done in one stroke. If you want to chalk leaves first, it must be done when the modelling paste is soft, and rubbed well in. Otherwise when you paint on the gum arabic you will wipe off the chalk at the same time. Store in an airtight container in the refrigerator and re-boil it when next required. It is advisable to make only a small amount at a time.

B   1 tsp gelatine
     1 tsp liquid glucose
     2 desertspoons water

Put the water in a cup or small container and sprinkle over the gelatine. When absorbed, stand in a pot of water and heat until dissolved. Add the liquid glucose, and stir well. Keep the mix warm while painting leaves. Store in sealed container in the refrigerator, and re-heat to use. Holly berries can also be dipped in shine for an extra glossy look.

C Alternately, paint on egg white. Use 2 coats, allowing the first to dry before applying the second. This method is not as long lasting as the Gum Arabic or Gelantine, and produces more a waxy look, rather than shine. It is suitable for flowers that have a waxy look.

Crowea with Holly leaves and berries.

77

Handy Hints

They say necessity is the mother of invention, and it's true. Pressure of work has forced me to find many shortcuts, and ways of eliminating waste. By passing them on, I hope I can save some decorators a few of the frustrations our craft bedevils us with.

HINTS ON COOKING CAKES

With the new fancy shaped tins, lining with paper or foil is tedious and not always successful. Try using a thick layer of LARD dusted with flour. Butter, margarine, or aerosol sprays are no substitute for lard when cooking fruit cakes. For security, you can line the base with a piece of commercial baking paper cut to fit. When the cake is cooked, remove from the tin immediately, turn the cake back on its base, and paint the top and sides with wine. Place in a plastic bag (to keep the moisture in, and stop the edges from going hard), wrap in a towel or newspaper and allow to cool slowly. Clean the tins with hot water only — no detergent — and they will be left with a fine coat of lard, which will protect them against rusting without the need to dry them in the oven. Tins used in this way stay bright and new looking.

Unused cake mix can be frozen for up to two months, then slowly thawed, and added to the next batch.

If you find that large cakes often overcook on the bottom or sides the problem is easily overcome. Place a thick slab of wood or chipboard in the oven, and sit your cakes on it. Heat the wood separately first to dispel any fumes, and if necessary cover the bottom and sides with foil. If the tops of your cakes burn, put the board on the shelf above, and if you have a "hot spot" on one side, position the board over it.

Another helpful hint is to use an extra thermometer in the oven, so you can see if one shelf is getting hotter, and adjust the temperature accordingly.

If you use the shallow American tins, and find cakes rising in the middle to form a hump, correct the problem by placing the tin inside a deeper Australian one — any shape tin will do the trick. This also applies to bell shaped tins.

HINTS ON COVERING CAKES

To easily cover a cake with almond icing, roll the paste out between two sheets of plastic. When you have the correct size, peel off the top piece. The plastic on the bottom allows you to lift the paste without splitting, and throw it over the cake — plastic uppermost of course. Rub and press the paste on to the cake before removing the top sheet of plastic, then finish smoothing in the usual manner.

If your almond paste is very crumbly, try adding a handful of plastic icing to it. An economical way of adding almond taste to a cake is to simply do away with the almond paste, and add a few drops of almond essence to your plastic icing. Work it in evenly, and cover the cake in the normal way.

To smooth icing on the sides of petal cakes, I use a short length of plastic pipe, which is just wide enough for my finger to fit down, and just a little longer than the height of an average cake. Slip your finger down the pipe and roll it round the cake. This method works well on the back of heart cakes, and the indentations on key cakes.

Always roll your plastic icing out on icing sugar — never cornflour. Once cornflour comes in contact with

moisture, such as a cake, it ferments. This is a prime cause of leaking, popping and splitting in covered cakes. It is wise to use pure icing sugar, as some softened types have cornflour in them to prevent hard lumps forming.

If your cake starts to leak or seep, then the damage has to be repaired. Use a sharp tool to cut away all the discoloured icing at the base of the cake, working until you are into clean icing. Repack the hole with moulding paste — not plastic icing. Give it time to dry, then pipe the border back on.

When covering a cake, it is easy to accidentally poke a dent in it with your finger, or a tool. A hot knife blade will usually help conceal your repair job.

HINTS ON COVERING BOARDS

Covering boards with fabric can be extremely effective, but a nightmare unless you observe two rules:
A   Always use fabric with some stretch, and
B   Always use aerosol glue to stick it down.
I generally buy white Jersey and dye it myself, remembering to dye any ribbon that's needed at the same time. To prevent the fabric from drawing the moisture out of the cake, and also preserve the appearance of the fabric board, cover it with plastic before sitting the cake on it. Hold it in place with a dob of royal icing on the top, and use tape to secure it underneath. Once the cake is covered, cut the plastic away from the cake with a scalpel.

Covering the underside of boards for tiered cakes is easy with white "Contact". It's neat and easy to wipe clean of any marks gained while decorating the cakes. If you use coloured backing, a soft blush of colour will reflect down on the cake below.

To smooth silver paper on boards, try using a childs chalk duster (blackboard eraser). I always pin a scrap of fabric over the duster. Any glue picked up can be washed off the cover, and the duster itself stays clean and soft.

HINTS ON PIPING

Egg white, and pure icing sugar (confectioners sugar), makes perfect royal icing. I have never found the need to add anything else. I use eggs straight from the refrigerator — by the time you have stirred it for fifteen minutes or so, it will be at room temperature. However, if you intend using anything less than an O tube, it is very necessary to put the icing sugar through an extremely fine sieve. I have used royal icing up to a week old for lace and extension work, but it needs to be beaten again for at least 15 minutes.

Piping bags last indefinitely, if you first line them with a plastic freezer bag. Use a pen or pencil, and push a corner of the plastic bag into the icing bag, and out the end. Cut away the protruding plastic, leaving enough to fold back over the union or screw. Attach your piping tube or nozzle over the plastic, but take care that the plastic bag doesn't twist as you do so, or you will cut off the icing flow. When you have finished piping, simply remove the plastic bag with the icing in it. If you secure both ends, the icing can be stored in the bag, completely safe from air, which would dry it out.

If you have a small amount of coloured piping to do, and find the correct amount won't be enough to give you a decent grip on your icing bag, try this idea:—
Line the piping bag with plastic, and put in your small amount of icing. Twist the plastic liner to seal off the royal icing, then put some more icing of whatever

colour is handy into another plastic bag, and drop it in on top of the first. Fold the outer bag over both bags, and presto, a little bit of icing that you can still get a grip on.

If you are only going to write a message, such as "Happy Birthday", then colour just enough icing to fill the tube only, and use whatever else is handy in the bag itself.

Should you have small amounts of coloured icing left around, then use it to make buds, berries or grapes, by dipping stamens in it.

You can also save your royal icing by freezing it, but remember to give it a really good beating when you do thaw it out.

Invisible joins in shell borders are a snap with this trick. Before commencing on the cake, pipe some extra shells on to the side of a surface from which they can be levered off when dry. Take care to make them the same size as you intend them to be on the cake. Now, simply pipe your shell edge as usual, and when there is room for only one more, take one of the dry shells, and slip the point under the first one, and press it over the tail of the last shell you piped. Once dry, the joins are impossible to see.

Piping lace, especially a lot of it, can be slow and very tiring on your hands. I have learnt to speed up the process by using both hands. Grip the piping bag with your left hand, then hold the nozzle or tube with your right hand as you would a pen. Now, simply squeeze with your left hand, and guide with your right. It will feel awkward at first, but if you persevere, you will find your lace improving, and your hands will be free of tension.

I use the same method for writing on cakes. However, I have another little trick that also helps. Provided your covering icing is nice and firm, use a ruler to gently draw a line with white chalk where you wish to write on the cake. Take care to use fresh chalk, which will make a line easily, without the need for pressure which could dent or leave a scratch. In a good light, you can use the line to keep your wording straight, and all the same height. Once the piping has dried, use a stiff paint brush to erase the chalk.

Lastly, I have seen many different ways of sticking ribbon round cakes, but have found you simply can't beat plain egg white, painted on with a fine brush.

HINTS ON FLOWER MAKING

To keep cut out flowers from drying before you can work them, try this hint. Glue a small piece of sponge on to the bottom of whatever you use to cover your flowers. In hot dry weather, slightly dampen the sponge, and the moisture will keep your icing workable.

For dusting with cornflour, tie a cup of cornflour into an old, clean, handkerchief, and secure with a rubber band. Use it to pat on your hands and board for a fine coating that will avoid large buildups of cornflour.

Paste left over after you have cut out some flowers is inclined to be dry, and harder to use. The simplest remedy is to mix a drop of water into it to counter the drying effect of the cornflour it was rolled out on.

If the weather is really hot and dry, and your paste is drying faster than you can work it, then a little plastic icing mixed with it usually helps.

I find cornflour the most successful for rolling out my moulding paste, but potato flour is excellent for mixing with chalks, and produces a much more even colour when you dust it on flowers.

If you are using soft plastic veiners on leaves, or petals, you can accentuate the veins by rubbing them with chalk before pressing on to your paste.

Royal icing on the backs of flowers such as heath and fuschia tends to grow air bubbles. The faster they dry, the less chance of this happening, so paint the backs of only ten or so at a time before putting them in a warm place to dry. My favourite place is the oven, with just the light on. This is a handy place to keep flowers before use during especially damp weather.

Recipes
Moulding Paste

250g icing sugar (8 ozs)
30ml water (1 oz)
2 scant teaspoons gelatine
1 rounded teaspoon liquid glucose

Sift icing sugar into a bowl. Measure water into a small bowl or cup and sprinkle with the gelatine. When it has been absorbed stand in a saucepan of hot water and dissolve gently. Once it has completely dissolved add the glucose. When the liquid is clear and free of any lumps add it to the icing sugar, stirring with a knife. Store the mixture in a plastic bag and seal in an airtight container. The mix needs to stand for about eight hours before use.

Stiffening

3 parts sugar
1 part water

Stir over heat until mix boils. Remove from heat immediately and continue stirring till all sugar grains have dissolved. Use while hot. Store in sealed container in refrigerator. Reheat before next use.

If you have a microwave, then you can make very small amounts and use it fresh each time (1 tsp of water to 3 tsp of sugar).

Embroidery

Embroidery

Lace

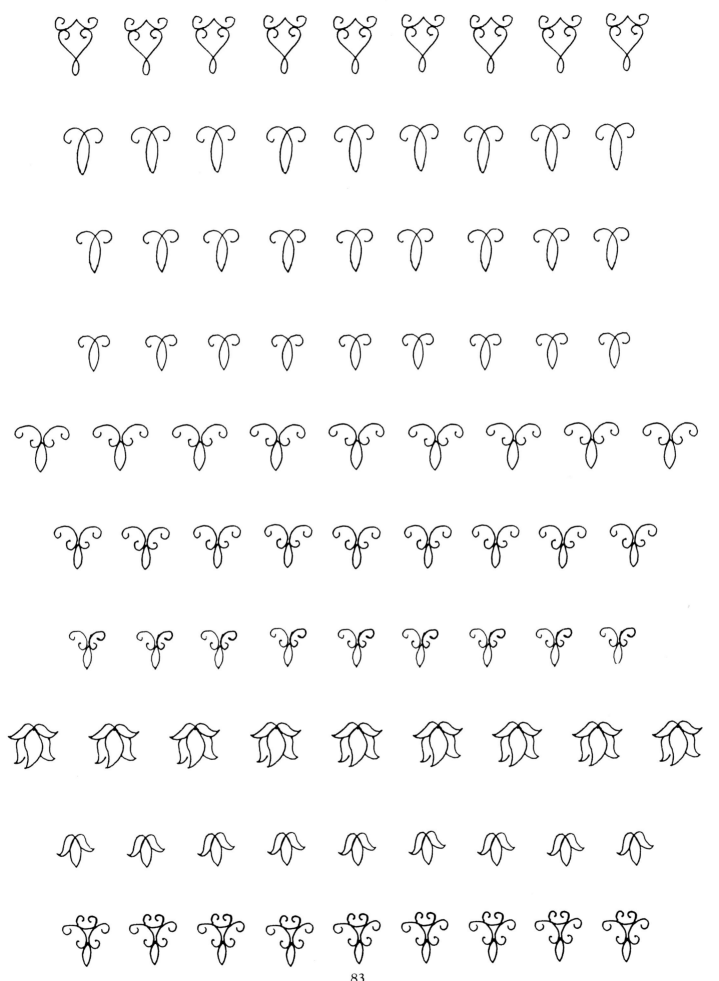

83